MUMBO JUMBO,
STAY OUT OF THE GUMBO

JOHNETTE DOWNING

ILLUSTRATED BY

JENNIFER LINDSLEY

PELICAN PUBLISHING COMPANY
GRETNA 2017

ISBN: 9781455623006
E-book ISBN: 9781455623013

Printed in China
Published by Pelican Publishing Company, Inc.
1000 Burmaster Street, Gretna, Louisiana 70053

For the animals of Louisiana —JD
To my students at Alice M. Harte Charter School
and to my son, Haden, always inspiring me every day —JL

It is Fat Tuesday,
and things are getting hot.
This *Courir de Mardi Gras*,
I will not be in the pot!

MUMBO JUMBO,
STAY OUT OF THE
GUMBO.

Le capitaine puts on
his *capuchon*.
Hey, alligator,
you better get gon'!

MUMBO JUMBO,
STAY OUT OF THE
GUMBO.

Cajun accordions play chank-a-chank.
Tous les crawfish, vacate that bank!

Ma mère and *mon père* are dancing a jig.
I better shake a feather to warn the pig!

MUMBO JUMBO,
STAY OUT OF THE
GUMBO.

Cooks stir a *roux* in every shack.
Listen up, oysters—stay in the sack!

Horseback riders stop at every home.
Turkeys in the field, you better roam!

Wagons of riders come pulled behind trucks.
There is not much time to warn the ducks!

MUMBO JUMBO,
STAY OUT OF THE
GUMBO.

This old prairie house is their next stop.
Make haste, rabbits! Hop, hop, hop!

MUMBO JUMBO,
STAY OUT OF THE
GUMBO.

The band is playing on the front stoop.
Oh *mais chère*, I better warn the coop!

MUMBO JUMBO,
STAY OUT OF THE
GUMBO.

Masked revelers run to and fro,
but all the animals are lying low.

MUMBO JUMBO,
STAY OUT OF THE
GUMBO.

They beg at each farm
and every house,
but there is nary a critter
from a gator to a mouse.

MUMBO JUMBO,
STAY OUT OF THE
GUMBO.

Onions, peppers, greens, and celery
are all they will have for their revelry.

MUMBO JUMBO,
STAY OUT OF THE
GUMBO.

Across Acadiana with no animals in sight,
all the Cajuns eat *gumbo z'herbes* tonight.

MUMBO JUMBO,
ENJOY YOUR GREEN
GUMBO.

AUTHOR'S NOTE

I root for the chicken! I enjoy the Courir de Mardi Gras: the music, costuming, celebration of community, cultural heritage, and traditions. The chasing of a real chicken—not so much. The Courir de Mardi Gras, known in Louisiana as "the chicken run," is an event that takes place on Fat Tuesday, the day before Ash Wednesday. Masked revelers, called the "Mardi Gras," travel from house to house across the Cajun prairie, ceremoniously begging for ingredients to make a communal gumbo as a celebration before the Catholic forty-day abstinence period of Lent.

Farmers offer onions, celery, and vegetables from their gardens to put into the soup, but the highlight of this rural Mardi Gras, for some, is when a farmer offers a chicken. The farmer releases the chicken and the revelers chase it around a farmyard until the chicken has been caught.

Over the years, the chasing of the chicken, in many areas, has become more symbolic and humane. Measures at certain chicken runs have been enacted to ensure the chicken is not harmed or overstressed.

As an animal lover, though admittedly not yet a vegetarian, I was inspired to write a Cajun Mardi Gras story with a twist, one in which the chicken outsmarts the revelers by warning all the animals to hide on Fat Tuesday. My goal, in writing this book, is to encourage the various Courir de Mardi Gras groups to consider more symbolic and humane ways of celebrating the chicken.

Further, I wanted to high-light a lesser-known, though equally delicious, type of vegetarian gumbo for my vegan friends who have been asking me to write at least one food book into which their children could sink their teeth. I hope you enjoy my original contribution to Cajun lore. Let's root for the chicken!

A MUMBO JUMBO OF WORDS

Capuchon—a pointed hat worn by Courir de Mardi Gras revelers; an adaptation of hats worn in earlier European carnival traditions.

Chank-a-chank—a term referring to Cajun music and, in particular, to its rhythmic foundation.

Courir de Mardi Gras—a French phrase meaning "the Fat Tuesday run"; a carnival celebration whereby masked and costumed men (and, increasingly, women) on horseback ride from house to house in Southwest Louisiana begging for ingredients to make a communal gumbo.

Fat Tuesday—in French, "Mardi Gras"; Fat Tuesday, the day before Ash Wednesday, is the actual day of carnival, which is preceded by a season of celebrations beginning on or after the Epiphany, or Kings' Day.

Gumbo—the West African word for "okra," gumbo is a roux-based soup. There are numerous varieties of gumbo, most of which include meat or seafood such as chicken, andouille sausage, duck, rabbit, turkey, alligator, shrimp, oysters, or crawfish.

Gumbo z'herbes—a roux-based soup made with a variety of leafy green vegetables and herbs but no meat. This dish is traditionally served on Good Friday during the Catholic observance of Lent.

Le capitaine—French words meaning "the captain"; refers to the leader of the Courir de Mardi Gras.

Mais chère—French words meaning "but friend."

Ma mère—French words meaning "my mother."

Mon père—French words meaning "my father."

Mumbo jumbo—a colloquial term meaning a jumble or a nonsensical idea.

Roux—flour that is browned in fat and is used as a thickening and flavoring agent in Cajun and Creole cooking.

T'fer—Cajun French term derived from the French words "petit fer" or "little iron." A t'fer, also known as a Cajun triangle, is a rhythmic musical instrument used in Cajun music.

Tous les—French words meaning "all the."

RECIPE FOR GUMBO Z'HERBES

Courtesy of Scott Billington

Sometimes written on New Orleans menus as Gumbo Zaire, this vegetarian gumbo is traditionally made by Catholics on Holy Thursday and served on Good Friday. It can be made as spicy as you like by adjusting the cayenne. For luck, many cooks believe that seven different types of greens should be used.

7 bunches of fresh greens, to total 3 pounds (beet greens, collards, kale, mustard, chicory, mizuna, watercress, carrot tops, Swiss chard, spinach, green cabbage)
⅔ cup high smoking point vegetable oil (canola or safflower are good)
⅔ cup all-purpose flour
2 medium onions, diced
1 green bell pepper, diced
2 ribs celery, diced
4 cloves garlic, finely diced
½ cup chopped parsley
⅛ tsp. cayenne, or to taste

¼ tsp. white pepper
¼ tsp. black pepper
1 bay leaf
Several sprigs of fresh thyme, chopped
Several sprigs of fresh marjoram, chopped
3 cloves, ground
3 allspice berries, ground
Salt and additional black pepper to taste
Filé (optional)
Hot sauce (optional)

Wash the greens thoroughly by submerging them in the sink to remove all dirt and grit. Remove the stems and tough parts. Toss the greens into a big pot with 2 quarts of boiling water. Drain them as soon as they are wilted, reserving the cooking liquid. Puree half the greens in a blender with some of the cooking liquid, in batches as required. When the remaining greens are cool enough to touch, chop them finely.

Make a roux by heating the oil in a cast-iron pan over a medium flame until it barely begins to smoke. Rapidly stir in the flour and continue stirring until the mixture turns chestnut brown, being careful not to burn it or splash it on you! Quickly stir in the onion, bell pepper, and celery and sauté them until they begin to caramelize. Add the garlic, parsley, and all the spices, and sauté for another five minutes.

In the big pot, combine the pureed greens, chopped greens, roux mixture, and enough cooking liquid to make a thick soup. Simmer over low heat for two hours, adding cooking liquid or water as required and taking care to stir frequently so the gumbo doesn't burn. Adjust the seasoning to taste.

Serve over rice, passing around the filé, hot sauce, and some warm French bread.

Serves 6-8